D1048145

# FROM ATHEIST TO BAHÁ'Í

## A JOURNEY THROUGH SUFFERING

SUSAN LIEBERMAN WALKER, PH.D.

THOUGHTFUL PUBLISHING COMPANY

SEATTLE

Copyright © 2013
Susan Lieberman Walker.
All rights reserved.

No portion of this document may be reproduced, copied, or distributed in any form whatsoever without the expressed written permission of the author and publisher.

THOUGHTFUL PUBLISHING COMPANY
321 10TH AVENUE SOUTH, #711
SEATTLE, WASHINGTON 98104

nufolk@bigplanet.com
509-594-6331

Cover Design:
Seth Walker – sethwalkerdesign.com

# ACKNOWLEDGEMENTS

I want to extend my love and thanks to my husband, David Edward Walker, for his loving encouragement, advice, and for surviving with me the experiences that so easily could have torn us apart. We faced our struggles together and allowed each other the space to grow and change. Thank you for being the friend of my dreams.

My love and appreciation to my two sons, Ben and Seth, their courage, their kindness, their compassion… watching you become two amazingly caring men has been such a privilege.

To my parents, Helen, Stan, and Joyce, and sister, Carole, who stood by me throughout this long journey with love, encouragement, support, and patience – thank you with all of my heart.

To our two dearest friends, Randie and Steve Gottlieb, who endured our cynical grilling as we learned about the Bahá'í Faith and have supported and encouraged us as we walk the path together, thank you. To our writer's group, the Haqiqats, thank you for creating a safe space in which to share my most painful memories as I put them into words. I treasure each one of you.

Thank you for your editing expertise – Dave, Randie, and Steve, and for the beautiful book cover, graphic designer extraordinaire - Seth Walker, whose designs can be found at www.sethwalkerdesign.com.

I also want to extend my thanks to two wonderful organizations – Families of SMA and the Muscular Dystrophy Association, both of which provide aid and support for families when they need it most. You have helped us maintain our hope and courage.

# TABLE OF CONTENTS

# MORE THAN MEETS THE EYE

God. The opiate of the masses. A creation by humankind to deal with the uncertainty of the physical world. An imaginary being to soothe humans in a random universe filled with suffering. An explanation for impermanence – to assist people in facing their own death. I accepted these ideas as truth. I couldn't see God; He didn't exist.

It was easy for me to live without God. All I had to do was rely on logic and myself. I grew up with Spock: logic above emotion; Ayn Rand and the virtue of self-interest, the immigrant credo, and the protestant ethic – pull yourself up by your own bootstraps. I alone was responsible for my achievements and my failures. To succeed in this world, I must work hard. I must do my best and get all I could out of this life because that is all there is. Once you're done, you're done. The American dream was built into my DNA. My parents were well - educated and able to take advantage of all society had to offer.

I obtained my education and got married. My husband and I started out small, saved our money, bought a dump of a house in an upcoming neighborhood and fixed it up with sweat and muscle. Property values increased, and we sold the house, making enough money to pay off our student loans. We bought a bigger house and a nice car with manageable payments. When we felt a need for community, we found a liberal church where the word 'God' was blotted out of the hymnals.

And then I faced an event that tore me apart…

When I was a child, I had this idea that when you died, you fell on your back and floated up to heaven. I could picture people all over the world floating up to heaven. This was before I found out that when you died, you were buried in the ground and lived on in the memories of those who loved you. It wasn't until I met my husband-to-be, a man whom I knew I would marry after our first long into-the-night talk, that the possibility of an 'other' world entered my mind. On one of our many intense dates where we talked about philosophy and life and meaning, my future husband, a curiously spiritual individual, took out tarot cards and did our first reading, one which seemed to map with uncanny accuracy our immediate future. I felt our destiny intimately tied together and that there was some strange, other-worldly purpose for our uniting. Unexplainable and completely illogical, something drew me to this man and a world of mystery.

After we had our first child, another clue revealed itself that there just might be more to this world than I could have ever conceived.

A lovely little boy of not more than two or three years, pointed toward the ceiling in the hall corner and asked, "Who dat? Who dat?"

"Where? Show me. "

"Dare. Dare. Who dat?"

Who or what was he seeing? Why couldn't I see?

We had a second child, another lovely little boy. One night after putting both of our children to bed, my husband and I were wakened from a sound sleep by a baby's cry. It was an unfamiliar voice. I tiptoed upstairs and found both boys fast asleep. Over the days and weeks, I continued to hear this strange wailing. I checked repeatedly, and this voice was not the cry of either of our boys. Did it come from outside? A neighbor? I knew all of the people around us. There were no babies visiting. The windows were closed, and it was winter.

I called my sister who for some peculiar reason believed in ghosts. She instructed me to do the following: when I was lying in bed and heard the crying, comfort the baby in my mind. Tell this baby that everything would be all right and imagine I was rocking and soothing the baby. My sister assured me the crying would stop. I did as my sister advised, and the crying stopped. Bizarre. I wasn't crazy. I hadn't been hearing things. My husband was a witness. He had heard this crying. What did it mean? My carefully constructed, logical world was becoming slightly frayed.

The next time I questioned whether there was more to this world than meets the eye was born out of tragedy. My youngest boy was just beginning to cruise the furniture and take his first steps. He was an explorer, speedily crawling around the house, up the stairs, on to the dishwasher door, back and forth to pull out plugs from the wall. He was very busy and always moving, fast, the kind of child who I thought, like his aunt, would jump up from the bath and run out of the door stark naked, a story repeatedly told about my fearless and bold sister as a child.

One day, however, this little ball of energy stopped pulling himself up to stand. He stopped taking wobbly steps before falling to his bottom. I thought, since he had started this at not more than eight or nine months, that he must have scared himself and wasn't quite ready. Very logical. But then his crawl seemed to get slower in the evenings as he crawled up the stairs to bed as I walked behind him. He must be tired. That's all. Then, he tried to crawl up on to the open door of the dishwasher and play with the rack, one of his favorite activities and something he did daily. He couldn't get his leg up. He struggled and struggled. In order to forestall his increasing frustration, I lifted him up and set him on the dishwasher door so he could play, but I knew... At that moment, I knew something was wrong, terribly wrong, and fear filled my body. I called my husband and described what happened. We made the first of what turned out to be many, many appointments.

*When suffering knocks at your door and you say there is no seat for him, he tells you not to worry because he has brought his own stool.* – Chinua Achebe[1]

# ONE OF THREE POSSIBILITIES

The pediatrician saw our son and sent him for x-rays – are his hips dislocated? No. We were sent to the rehabilitation physiatrist. Our little boy crawled up and down the hall while the doctor and a group of her medical students watched and commented under their breath. Something was wrong. His movements were unusual. His reflexes weren't responding properly. What was it? What was wrong? Go to a neurologist for more tests.

The neurologist said it was a neurological disease and would result in one of three possible outcomes: fatal, untreatable but not fatal, or treatable. It was April. We were scheduled to go on vacation for a week to see my father and step-mother on the California coast. Should we cancel the trip? The neurologist told us to go; a week wouldn't make a difference, and he would complete the testing for a definitive diagnosis when we returned. We went with fear gripping every muscle in our bodies but pretending everything was fine because we had these two beautiful boys, full of energy and laughter, curiosity and awe, loving life and being alive. We went to California.

On the plane, as I was holding my youngest in my arms, I prayed for the first time in my life. Not to God. I didn't believe in God. But I prayed to my ancestors, my grandma Anna and grandpa Lou, my great-grandma Minnie and great-grandpa George. I asked them to protect my child, to help make everything okay. Why did I do this? I didn't even believe in an afterlife. Did fear make me turn to something I couldn't see and to a power I hoped would make things better, like calling for my mom to comfort me when I woke from a bad dream? Now, I was the parent. Who could I turn to? It didn't make any sense to me, but I imagined my ancestors in a circle, picturing them like skydivers floating in that imagined heaven of my childhood, holding hands against a starry sky, encircling my child, protecting him, making sure he would be all right.

How did I carry on with fear pervading every cell in my body? How did I pretend everything was just like it was the week before, the month before?

The visit was filled with silent anguish, the waiting to find out, the waiting to find out the world would end. But we carried on. We had two bubbly children. That is what kept us sane. Playing with our children, exploring the beach, catching tiny crabs scurrying under the sand as the tide went out, the salt water waves reaching up to their outstretched toes. Building sand castles, two-lane roads in the sand for the tiny cars and trucks.

My husband and I would frequently catch one another's eyes over the heads of our children in silent communications, understanding the dread that each of us was gripped with, the horror of what we both knew was to come. The world surrounded us as though nothing was wrong. In these moments, we clung to each other like life rafts, knowing we had no control over the storm battering us or the direction the wind would fling us.

I called my mom to check in. My mom, who was a psychiatrist and had some knowledge of neurology, had been reading old neurology textbooks to try and find out what kind of disease her grandson might have. She told me to look at his hands when they were resting. Did his fingers jump and twitch as though in spasm? If they did, she said, that would be 'the bad one,' – fatal.

We left the beach and stopped at the drug store. My husband and our oldest boy, now going on four and cute as a button, went into the store as our youngest slept in his car seat. I turned around to look at my sleeping son's hands and saw them twitching as he peacefully slept, blissfully unaware of the implications of the tiny spasms in his fingers.

I turned away and closed my eyes.

It was only through sheer force of will, using every ounce of strength I had, that I could maintain my composure and put a smile on my face as my husband and older son returned from the store.

I held my breath as though the very act of breathing would splinter the fragile threads that held me together. I would keep it together for my husband and my children.

No one would know.

*Deep, unspeakable suffering may well be called a baptism, a regeneration, the initiation into a new state.* – George Eliot[2]

# THE VOICE

That night as I lay in bed, I allowed terror to consume me. I felt like I was shattering into tiny shards strewn across the vast universe, imploding, exploding. My world was coming to an end, and silent screams of anguish echoed in my head, consuming and devouring me, endless and timeless. My son would die.

Abruptly, mysteriously, and opposing all logic and sense, cutting like a knife through my chaos and fear, came an image and a voice in my mind. The image seemed to be... who?

I thought he looked like a monk wearing a brown robe, unbelted and stretching down to his feet. A hood shadowed his face. His face. I had a sense that he was a male presence. I couldn't see his face, but I heard his voice.

Clearly, unmistakably, he said, "He will be teased in the schoolyard, and he will be married."

My terror ended, the fear subsided, and I dropped off to sleep.

I woke the next day, a bit calmer, but feeling I was just one day closer to the inevitable diagnosis. Of course, I remembered the voice from the night before, the words that reassured me, but I was a psychologist, for heaven's sake; I knew what a masterful instrument the mind can be, and how it has the power to protect, to ensure one's survival.

I also knew about hallucinations. Was I going crazy? Was my mind helping me survive this disaster by creating an image, a voice? I relied on my training and knew this was all probable. However, I also knew with a certainty that was disconcerting and troubling, that the voice was not 'of' me. Yet don't people in the throes of psychosis believe that the voices are coming from outside of their heads?

No, it did not come from my mind, I argued with myself. I knew I did not create it. I knew this.

The voice was another kink in my armor of certainty.

*To live is to suffer, to survive is to find some meaning in the suffering.* – Friedrich Nietzche[3]

# THE DIAGNOSIS

I had no recollection of the many events from the days just prior to sitting in the neurologist's office, waiting. The voice I'd heard a week before ("He will be teased in the school yard, and he will be married") was gone, replaced with my growing panic and feelings of utter helplessness, the only emotions that I experienced in that moment while I watched the doctor carefully place needles into our precious child's muscles, his legs, his arms as he screamed and screamed.

The doctor was checking to see whether the muscle nerves fired properly. My child could have no pain killer, nothing to interfere with the detection of nerve signals. I tried to comfort him, but there was no comfort to be had.

The doctor finally finished, left the room, and returned with the awful news. Our boy had Werdnig-Hoffman's disease. Yes, I had known that was a possibility. This was the fatal one; the disease that killed children before they turned two years old - the ALS of childhood (Lou Gehrig's disease). Children slowly lose muscle function until pneumonia makes it impossible for them to breathe. This was the disease that would take my son.

The doctor said he would refer us to the Muscular Dystrophy clinic. He looked at us with sorrowful eyes and let us walk out of the room. No one was there to catch us or to prevent us from collapsing in horror on the floor. No trained social worker helped us figure out how to now put one foot in front of the other. My husband and I left the room and walked down the long corridors of the hospital out to our car. We didn't speak. We barely breathed. We didn't know what to do.

When one of us finally was able to find our voice, I don't remember who it was, him or me, the question was asked – where should we go? We couldn't go to his family – they all lived in other states; we couldn't go to my family, my father and step-mother lived across the country, my sister and mom were at work. We stood by the car as our son slept in his stroller, exhausted from the crying and the pain. It was a bright April day, so sunny, so clear, a beautiful Michigan spring day.

Finally, one of us said – church; we would go to our church, the church that had God blotted out of the hymnals and the like-minded people where we went every Sunday to try and give our children some sort of community life and education about religion. We had a plan. We picked up our oldest son, who was only four years old, at the sitter's house and headed to the church. The minister wasn't there, but the music director, secretary, and a few other people gathered in his office while my husband and I told them the news. Toys were brought for our two boys as they laughed and played on the floor, oblivious to what was going on.

How could this be? I thought. Look at him; he doesn't look like he's dying. He's so alive and so filled with light and love and wonder.

What should we do now? We appealed to our church friends: tell us what to do. The music director, a woman with unforgettably striking red hair, suggested we take these two beautiful boys to the zoo. They are two curious, excited, and energized boys. Have a wonderful day, she said. Enjoy your family. Be together. Laugh, eat, see the animals, ride the zoo train. Have fun today. You will figure out what to do tomorrow. But today, go to the zoo.

I remember walking around the zoo that day, clutching on to my husband's hand, the cherry blossoms in bloom, the boys laughing at the giraffes, our oldest running about, our youngest pointing and smiling, directing where the stroller should go with his 'look!' and 'dere!' We rode the zoo train, and the boys were gleefully happy. They loved transportation; anything with wheels and sounds and motion.

It was a wonderful day, the only thing we could have done that day. We survived. Our boys were content. We made it through that unspeakable day.

The next week was a blur. People called and visited. Food filled the refrigerator. It was interesting that those closest to us were absent; friends who had been on the periphery of our lives came and took care of us. Was it too painful for those who were closest to us? Some took the boys to play so we could privately cry and my husband could pray, only to cover our faces with smiles and excitement when the boys returned.

I don't know how we continued, but we did. What choice did we have? The world kept on turning. It doesn't stop for someone's pain.

My mother knew a neurologist whose waiting list was months and months long, yet she was able to get us an appointment for a week later. A second opinion was needed. Was this death sentence final? Was there no reprieve, no second chance? We took our son to see the new doctor, hopeless and expecting confirmation of the sentence delivered by the first neurologist.

The doctor sat down in the room, smiling at us and watching our son crawl around, playing with the toys on the floor.

"Why so glum?" he asked.

"Our son has Werndig-Hoffman's disease… we were told that he won't live past age two…"

"No. That's ridiculous. Your son is going to go to college. He'll live a long life."

"What? What? Oh my God. What?"

The doctor explained that our son had Spinal Muscular Atrophy, type II. In his opinion, the other doctor had misdiagnosed him with the most severe form, type I. Babies with type I are born with very little muscle tone, he explained, and usually can't roll over let alone crawl or stand up. Our son was not going to die within six months, he affirmed. He would live. He would always use a wheelchair, but he would live.

He would live! The world shifted. We were given a reprieve from our week spent in hell.

My husband was convinced that his prayers had been answered. God had answered his prayers. He felt the future was changed by a miracle. I thought the first doctor made a horrible, almost criminal, mistake at our expense. I didn't believe this change was a miracle. I didn't believe it was because of God that my son would live or would go to college! I believed it was because of one doctor's foolish ignorance. But I was so, so grateful. So relieved. The world was different now. My son would live.

*We shall draw from the heart of suffering itself the means of inspiration and survival.* – Winston Churchill

# A REPRIEVE

With my young son, I was sucked into a new world of disability – appointments, doctors, physical therapists, occupational therapists, support groups, nurses, educational specialists, equipment dealers...

In this new world, I met families with children in so much worse shape than my son. At a state-run preschool for disabled children which provided the services of various therapists, my child was an anomaly. He could talk, learn, and even stand in braces. He would go to college!

The other mothers' children had a myriad of diseases I had never heard of; their children could not talk, could learn very little, and likely would not survive. These mothers clung together and made no room for me. To them, my son was the picture of health compared to their children.

During each of my son's classes with the therapists, I

left alone and went to one of my favorite restaurants, Elias Brothers' Big Boy, where I had my special treat: strawberry pancakes. My solace. Strawberry pancakes. I passed my time silently, alone. And still, I was grateful every day. My son would live.

My husband and I tried a support group, but we were the only parents with a child without a death sentence. The children of the other parents present had Duchenne's disease. Their children would become progressively weaker, likely ending up in wheelchairs while still in elementary school and dying in their twenties. How could we go and talk about our own trauma and pain with these people, knowing our son would live? I was grateful every day, yet I left the meeting in shame for my gift.

Although I was grateful, so grateful, at night I couldn't keep despair at bay. My son would never walk, run, climb trees, skip, jump, do cartwheels, play capture the flag, hike mountains, play tag with his brother, participate in track, soccer, little league, snow ski, water ski, tip toe, square dance.

The verbs, all the verbs, he would never do all the things I imagined this busy, active boy with boundless energy would love to do.

Why??? Why??? Would he date, would he marry? Would anyone love him forever? What would happen to my precious son?

Then, with a gasp, I remembered the voice, "He will be teased in the school yard, and he will be married."

I thought about the voice I had heard. Now I knew my son would live. Could the voice have known that the first diagnosis would be wrong? Did the voice really know what would happen in the future?

I thought about the words. Strange words: 'Teased in the school yard.' I would never say 'school yard' in my own speech. I would say 'playground.' From where did this word, 'schoolyard,' originate? It's such an old word and from a different time. And 'he will be married.' Could this be true?

I grasped onto these words, repeating them endlessly. They would be my lifeline as the years passed. And still, I didn't believe in God. I didn't understand the voice, but I didn't think it had anything to do with a God.

Until that night.

There was one particular night of despair and hopelessness, of aloneness and emptiness. I cried for my son and the pain he would bear, knowing how he would watch from his chair while others did what he wanted to do, knowing the heartache he would suffer from discrimination and prejudice. I cried for my husband's agony and suffering, knowing there was no way I could help soothe him. I cried for my oldest son whose family was irreparably changed. No running, no chasing his little brother.

I cried for my own helplessness, being unable to make anything right, to help my family, to heal the damage already done. I lay on my back in the dark room, my husband asleep beside me, and I cried.

Until that moment.

Until in front of the dark blackness before my closed eyes appeared millions of bright, glowing orbs. I jabbed at my closed eyes and turned my head back and forth. Where were the lights coming from? Not from the room around me. I stared at countless orbs stretched out into the distant blackness as far as I could see.

I watched silently, in wonder, now understanding. Without words, I knew that the orbs were souls, comforting me, letting me know I was not alone, that I never would be alone in my despair. I stared in wonder at these glowing orbs, exuding love and comfort.

Suddenly, startlingly, behind these millions of glowing orbs, the blackest of curtains, hiding the activity on the stage beyond, cracked open and a brilliant light shot forth, radiantly colorful, the most beautiful spectacle I had ever seen. The crack closed, and the light disappeared, yet it opened again in another spot.

Again, dazzlingly luminous light poured out, colors stark and unblemished in their most spectacular essence. I gazed in wonder and awe. The curtain closed and opened again in another spot. This happened again and again, and I knew with a certainty that astounded me — this was God.

The immense, unknowable, unimaginable beauty, suffused with unspeakable love was God. I was given a glimpse of this immensity. There was a God. Struck with this new knowledge, I watched the vision unfold before my eyes, mute with reverence and astonishment.

With my newfound understanding, I also knew God was not changing reality for me. My son would not be miraculously cured, yet I would never be left alone to face the struggles and heartache. God would always be there for me.

I now believed in God with every fiber of my being.

From uncompromising atheist to devout believer in a split second. How perfectly wonderful, I thought, that God showed me in the only way I could have ever come to believe. I had to be figuratively punched in the stomach so hard that I could not disregard or rationalize the experience. God showed me in the only way I could ever accept – through my own senses. It had to be tangible, something I could actually see.

I now knew there was a God… and I smiled.

*Let a teacher wave away the flies*

*And put a plaster on the wound.*

*Don't turn your head. Keep looking*

*At the bandaged wound. That's where*

*The light enters you.*

*And don't believe for a moment*

*That you're healing yourself.*

-- Rumi[5]

# NOW WHAT?

All the questions bubbled up.

What would I do with this God? How does one live with a God? What does it mean to believe in God? And if there is a God, why is there so much suffering in the world? How can God allow his creations to starve and hurt? Why is there such inequality; some have so much, others have so little. How does God explain all this?

And religions. Religion is supposed to be a path toward God. Why is there such hypocrisy? The abusive priests, the war on the nonbelievers, conversions through war and death. The spewed hatred: if you are not one of us, you will die and go to hell, to live in eternity in fire. We are the chosen, the few, only we will be saved. Groups of people separated and alienated by belief in a spiteful, vengeful God.

Everything I had heard told me religion was vile, used for evil, power, gathering riches, fame, and the oppression of others. Girls covered from head to toe so as not to tempt men who had no self-control, stay dumb and uneducated, remain slaves and servants. Death to all who don't believe.

I didn't understand. How could there be this unfathomable power of love that I knew God to be while organized religion seemed to undermine His message, projecting the very opposite of the loving, warm embrace I had felt that special night?

I brought up the question of suffering with my friends and acquaintances. I asked, why is there so much of it in the world? Why is it seemingly so random? Why would my youngest son never walk, my oldest never get to chase or wrestle with his little brother? My son is an innocent child – the God I knew wouldn't punish him. Did I commit some unforgivable sin for which I must pay through the suffering of my husband and sons?

On the other hand, I knew I lived in a world with doctors, therapists, insurance, and wheelchairs, all of the best that medicine had to offer, while a child in another part of the world might never have the opportunity to ride down the street in a battery-operated, toy four-wheeler, moving and steering and playing with the other kids.

I knew families with children who had much worse diagnoses than my son received. I knew families who had lost their children, suffering beyond belief. I knew I had enough food and a family, a job, education, home, and cars. I knew I was wealthy beyond belief in relation to most of the world. None of this made any sense to me.

God – answer these questions. Why is there so much suffering, and why does it seem to be related to an accident of birth? Why do some have so much and some have so little? Why is there prejudice and discrimination which both cause and amplify suffering? When and how will it stop? I had so many questions and wondered if I looked again, this time more closely at religion now that I believed in God, would I find my answers.

I began with the religion of my grandparents, Judaism. I accepted the beliefs of Judaism – there is only one God, the prophet brought teachings to the Jewish people, and the Ten Commandments are essential laws for us to follow for mankind to live peacefully and prosper. Suffering was understood in two ways; first, the result of a deserving punishment – "*God is exacting with His close ones to a hair's breadth*!"[6] Alternately, it could be seen as producing some future positive benefit. Both scenarios were unthinkable. What did my husband, my sons, or I do to deserve this punishment. If one of us did do something deserving punishment, how would we be able to correct the mistake if the crime was unknown to us? And what good could possibly come from this?

I struggled with stories in the Old Testament – the creation of the world in seven days? Was that supposed to be taken literally? I read about the differences of opinion in the

Jewish world about evolution versus literal creationism. Noah's Ark, David and Goliath – children's stories. Were these to be understood as metaphors? I remembered the stories from my childhood of Moses leading the chosen people to the Promised Land. Why were the Jews the chosen people? That would seem to be an accident of birth. I read the many laws of Judaism, most of which made sense for the time period to which they applied. This religion was over 3000 years old. It all seemed so distant to me, lacking relevance for my world today, and it did not speak to my need to see humanity as one, to know my son would be included as a vital member of the world community.

I quickly ruled out the Catholic Church. I could not accept the concept of Hell, that someone who did not accept the Gospel of Christ upon death would be eternally damned to separation from God. Eternal was a long, long time. I could not accept the idea of confessing my sins yearly to another person, and I did not understand the power of the priest to forgive one's sins. The ritual of Holy Communion confused me, and I could not separate my knowledge of the corruption of the papacy and the priesthood from the beauty of what I knew of Christ's teachings.

I thought about the Christians, the Mormons, the Jehovah Witnesses, all the myriad sects and splinter groups of Christianity. He is the only way. Through Him you will find salvation. But what about before Jesus? Does that mean that everyone who existed before Jesus was destined to Hell? What about the people who lived isolated and never had the chance to hear His words? What about the babies who died before baptism?

In Islam, I discovered that there was no concept of original sin; all people are born free of sin. Each person asks for forgiveness for transgressions directly through prayer to Allah without a middleman to forgive.

I was surprised to learn that 'jihad' meant to overcome internal struggles, to strive for social justice, and to overcome oppressive tyranny – not to kill nonbelievers. Women were equal to men in Islam. The religion of Islam had been subverted by tribal customs, fanaticism, greed, and power. I saw the beauty in the teachings, yet I could not accept that Muhammad would be the last and final prophet for all of humanity's existence. That did not make any logical sense. The laws set down for living 1500 years ago could not in their totality apply to a world thousands of years in the future. I understood man to be part of the evolution of the planet and was hoping that we would continue to evolve as we learned and matured. I saw the progression of prophets from Abraham to Moses to Jesus to Mohammed. Why would God send help to man from the beginning and then all of a sudden stop providing guidance?

I turned to Eastern religions – my husband read me stories from Buddhist writings, parables, and fables from which I was to extract wisdom. I didn't get it. I understood the basic truths about suffering, the Noble Eightfold Path, the basic rules of conduct, and the benefits of meditation to bring one towards detachment and enlightenment, but where was God in all this? I believed in God and was looking for help to understand God through religion. My husband believed in God and was a practicing Buddhist even though he struggled with the contradiction between the two sets of beliefs. I needed something that was cohesive, unified, a whole that I could grasp on to.

I was convinced that God would never leave one individual without a way to Him. What was that way? I concluded that today's organized religions were surely not the answer.

I turned to New Age spirituality. I joined a prayer circle with some of my spiritual women friends. We met weekly, discussed spiritual ideas, and grappled with questions about suffering. I learned about Qi gong, how to do Reiki, about earth religions and nature, accessed my own inner animal guides, read books such as *Conversations with God* and *The Celestine Prophecy*. I tried *A Course in Miracles* for daily teachings in how to live and understand God; I read Deepak Chopra, Caroline Myss, and Marianne Williamson. But I could not find the foundation of logic and reason in these writings. The messages for how to live, ways of being, and solutions to individual problems were there. Yet I was looking for something like 'the physics of everything' and couldn't find it in the New Age movement. If there was one Creator for the universe, then everything should be unified, connected. These writings didn't explain the whole picture, the coherence and unity of God and humanity, soul and spirit, suffering and joy, planets and stars, microbes and galaxies, the purpose of life and death. How could I integrate my reasoning mind with my new-found beliefs?

Did I have to negate a part of myself in order to believe in God?

*All that I say is, examine, inquire. Look into the nature of things. Search out the grounds of your opinions, the for and against. Know why you believe, understand what you believe, and possess a reason for the faith that is in you.* – Frances Wright[7]

# COINCIDENCE?

My husband and I journeyed to New Jersey for seven weeks to have our youngest participate in an experimental drug study. During our drive as we discussed our doubts and fears about committing to this study, subjecting our son to daily infusions and uprooting our family for the summer, we found ourselves following a truck with the name 'Takeuchi' written in giant letters across the back. Takeuchi was the name of the Japanese doctor who pioneered the use of this drug with SMA (Spinal Muscular Atrophy) kids. Dr. Takeuchi was the doctor whom our American doctor visited in Kyoto, Japan to discuss with him the possibility of doing a similar study in the U.S. We were following Dr. Takeuchi, his methods were being replicated, and our son was one of nine children in the United States study. Here was a truck with Dr. Takeuchi's name that we were directly behind, following toward New Jersey.

Was this a random coincidence? How was I to understand this kind of phenomenon? I had never seen the name Takeuchi other than on correspondence with the doctor and in his published research articles. Takeuchi on the back of a truck? Strange! And it was directly in front of us.

Very close in time, passing us on the right, came a huge tractor-trailer truck with G.O.D. splayed across the side. What was that? How could this kind of synchronicity occur? G.O.D? GOD?

More questions added to my confusion about God. What are coincidences? Are such occurrences meaningless, random events in the world into which the mind tries to inject meaning? Are they signs, spiritual events to which we must pay attention to learn from and gain understanding or knowledge? Are they confirmations, support for actions taken or paths followed?

During our stay in New Jersey, my husband commuted back and forth by air, spending weekends with us. One mild summer evening when I was alone while my children played with another family, I went outside and walked through the hotel grounds, looking up at the stars and feeling alone, desperate for the drug to show promise and help my son.

As I walked, I suddenly felt a rush of warmth and love surround me. I wrapped myself in this wonderful feeling.

The next day, I spoke to one of the women in my spiritual group who asked, "Did you feel it? We prayed for you and sent you love. Did you feel it last night?"

*Tell your heart that the fear of suffering is worse than the suffering itself. And that no heart has ever suffered when it goes in search of its dreams, because every second of the search is a second's encounter with God and with eternity.* -- Paulo Coelho[8]

# A NEW PATH

I had treasured my work as a psychologist – helping families, children, and individuals find their voices, search for answers already inside of them,  bring out their gifts and talents. I had partnered with them to find the strength to overcome forces, both internal and external, that impeded their growth.

But so much in my world had changed.  I heard a life-altering voice; I had a life-changing vision; I believed in God now.

How could I continue to be a psychologist if I knew that were I to walk into a colleague's office, they would think I was a wounded woman whose mind created these strange hallucinations? If someone had walked into my office six months earlier, describing such experiences, I would have thought the same. (I was not just a psychologist but an atheist, after all.) Visions and God did not correspond with the theories on which I based my work.  I couldn't conceive of a way to integrate my beliefs and theoretical orientation with such strange, mystical experiences. The two were mutually exclusive.

And most painfully, my ability to listen with warmth, understanding, and compassion to my patients had become compromised. I could no longer bear to listen to people complaining about their jobs, their unruly kids, their frustrations and dissatisfactions with life. I felt unable to come outside of myself, put myself in others' shoes as my family and I struggled to come to grips with our own suffering. My wounds were too fresh. I kept thinking as I listened to my patients – at least you have your health, at least you have a job, at least your child is healthy. As these thoughts broke through into my normally compassionate and empathic ear, I knew it was time to close my psychology practice.

But what would I do? I needed some work outside of the home, a way to contribute, something that would allow me flexibility to be available to take care of my children. I had to be able to take my youngest to therapies, go to planning meetings at his school, do daily stretches to lessen his contractures from sitting for long periods in his wheelchair, research new treatments, maintain all of the variety of medical equipment we'd acquired, not to mention just be a mom and play, read, teach, and explore the world with both of my children.

Because of the special needs of my youngest, I worked hard to make sure I remained available to my oldest son. Encouraging his interests, my husband and I took him to t-ball games, participated in Boy Scouts with him, built and organized massive Lego creations with him, and built trains that ran throughout the living and dining rooms.

My oldest son loved playing in the mud, and for his birthday, we arranged to have a dump truck bring a load of dirt (which would later be used for landscaping) for a mud birthday. On a hot Michigan summer day, friends in bathing suits came, a hose was turned on, and toy trucks and cars made a highway patchwork on the mound of dirt. Hidden prizes were found, gummy worm cupcakes were devoured, and mud-covered children rolled in the dirt. It was a birthday that for several years became a wonderful tradition.

I loved being a mom, and as my sons went to school, I became involved in the school community, volunteering in the classroom, going to PTA meetings, becoming friends with moms of my sons' classmates. I valued the atmosphere in our neighborhood school: open classrooms, children moving through different activities, hands-on exploration, watching the freedom and joy in discovery. The classrooms were full of wonderful energy and enthusiasm; they were exciting and vibrant learning environments. That is what I would do – I would become a teacher. I would be on my children's schedule and be home when they were home. I could help many children at a time in a different way rather than one at a time as a psychologist. I decided to become a teacher.

At that time in Michigan, the only way for me to become a teacher was to return to school and get another bachelor's degree. Psychology was not considered a 'teachable' major. I called every school in the state to see if I could go through a teaching certificate program since I already had a Ph.D. In the state of Michigan, this was impossible without returning to school for years.

My dreams were dashed. I could not rationalize the expense or time to go back to school and complete another degree. I was at a loss. My psychology practice was now closed, we were struggling on one income, and I felt that I had come to a dead end. Now what?

Meanwhile, my husband had become very dissatisfied with the direction of his own career. In his daily meditation, he had been praying for guidance for a new path. He wanted to be of greater service to humanity and wasn't sure of the direction he should take. Then, suddenly, a new opportunity presented itself. My husband accepted a job as a psychologist for the Indian Health Service in Washington State. We packed up and moved across the country to a small town in rural eastern Washington.

As soon as we had landed in our new home, I called the local university and discovered that, unlike Michigan, I could be accepted into a part-time teacher certification program. In fact, I was able to get an emergency substitute certificate and immediately begin working in schools while taking classes toward my teaching certificate, which I would have in only two years' time.

The doors were swiftly opened for me to change career paths. Was all this coincidental? Did God have a hand in turning a roadblock into an open speedway? My husband's prayers were seemingly answered. Were my unspoken prayers answered as well?

However, settling into this new community was not an easy task.

*Suffering has been stronger than all other teaching... I have been bent and broken, but – I hope – into a better shape. –* Charles Dickens[9]

# SUFFERING

I kneeled on the bed in our new home in Washington state, staring out the window, seeing the crisp manicured lawns, the well-kept ranch houses, the cul-de-sac, the subdivision. No one was outside. This neighborhood was completely silent.

I thought about the people engaged in activities, each in their own homes, each alone. I looked beyond the neighborhood, up the hill at the houses dotting the landscape where the wealthiest people lived in magnificent gated estates, the doctors, lawyers, business owners, orchard and landowners, fruit company owners. I thought of what money had bought them – each person, separate, alone, isolated, disconnected. I thought about the pain and suffering in each of the homes, in each of the hearts, people filling their time with meaningless activity, belongings, anything to dull the pain.

I thought about my children at the elementary school

down the street, sitting in the cafeteria eating silently. No talking was allowed during lunch – the only way the staff felt they could ensure the students would eat, the only way to ensure control over the 'unruly' kids. I thought about my children's attempt to make contact, to make friends in this new, closed community they had moved into crossing the country – no way in. They were newcomers, facing painful struggles to find a friend, to fit in. Desks lined up in neat columns, workbooks open, fill-in-the-blank.

I thought of my oldest son being torn away from his very best friend, his kind heart and gentle spirit, too good for this world. I thought of my youngest son, his spirit shining so brightly, encircling all he came in contact with, yet his body stuck in his wheelchair.

I thought of attending our first Indian ceremonies and community gatherings, my husband off talking to his new friends and acquaintances while the kids and I sat silently, trying to smile, keeping our eyes down, trying to follow the native customs, reaching out – the only white people in the midst of this new and strange culture – learning about what it means to be a minority, at that time feeling alienated and unwelcome before opening our hearts and being joyfully included. We seemed to be again, always learning what it means not to belong.

I thought about the horribly disturbing letters to the editor in the town's local paper—vicious, hate-filled letters about the Mexican interlopers who came to take away resources from the community, about the Indians, called good-for-nothings, lazy, drunk again.

I thought about the migrant workers who came to pick apples, stayed, raised children who now made up fifty percent of the school district but remained in poverty, children interpreting for their parents, or families that followed the crops, kids staying in school for a season until they moved again.

I thought of my husband, desperately trying to make a difference and being undercut, shot down, alone, and so lonely in his work. The psychologist who was not wanted, rejected by his colleagues. What are you doing here? Brought on board by higher-ups without any input from his department. Hated before he walked in the door.

I thought of our rez dog, Tumna, whom we brought home to try and add life and joy to the emptiness; a dog who belonged with his pack, running free on acres of land, but was now a suburban dog being walked on a leash.

I thought of my own bitter emptiness and loneliness. I thought of my own inept attempts to befriend the mothers and teachers at my kids' school. I thought about having walked alone from the broken down van on the highway, no one to call and miles to walk before I could get to the school to pick up the kids.

I thought of the immensity of the task before us – to make a difference in the world, to connect, to find a purpose and meaning. To raise our children in a world that would be worth living in. I knew I couldn't do it. I knew I wouldn't ever actually do something, but I thought about it. I thought about it. Take the whole family out of the pain of living in this world. Car crash down the mountain pass. One swerve. Easy.

I thought of all this and through my tears, I begged God, "Show me! Show me how to live in our world. Show me how to raise my children in a world like this. I can't do this, God. I can't do it. Show me. Show me how to live."

*There is an ancient tribal proverb I once heard in India. It says that before we can see properly we must first shed our tears to clear the way.* – Libba Bray[10]

# GOD SHOWED ME

As a substitute teacher, I rarely worked in one school for more than a day at a time, rotating through each school in the district, getting to know their different atmospheres, student populations, teachers and their philosophies and styles of teaching. I learned how unlike one school was from the next and was fortunately able to find the environment that would best fit my children and their own learning styles, transferring them to this new school with both an elementary and middle school, so they could stay together. It was a warm environment with classrooms filled with activity, hands-on projects, and engaged children who were discovering and learning.

One Monday, I subbed in an elementary school and was required to take my class to an assembly. Dutifully following the teacher's lesson plans, I escorted my students, made sure they were sitting quietly, and settled myself in to watch the show. The Diversity Dance Workshop, a group of high school kids from all over the world, began their presentation of a series of dances showing the destructive effects of inequality, prejudice, the extremes of wealth and poverty, racism and sexism, drugs and alcohol, and disunity.

I watched in awe, forgetting to attend to the students in my charge and, when it was over, felt thankful that they had remained quiet and attentive. The dancers' movements expressed the power of healing in unity, compassion, and oneness. Their dances astounded me, and I went home that day with a measure of hope for the future of humanity.

Tuesday, I subbed in another school and was surprised when I read the lesson plans for the day and discovered that I was to take this class to an assembly. Could it be the same one I had seen the day before? It was, and I watched with greater attention, looking closely at the faces of the dancers, seeing optimism and confidence as they enacted the world's problems and performed the solutions.

By Wednesday, my third day that week subbing in yet a different school which hosted the Diversity Dance Workshop, I knew that these youth would change the world; they had shared something important, something powerful, and something everyone needed to see. I wondered if the elementary school children who made up the audiences in the three schools understood the life-changing ideas they had witnessed. I went home and told my husband, "You *have* to see these dancers. They will change the world!"

The dancers were performing at the Unitarian Church that Sunday, and my husband went to see them. He was impressed as well and immediately set about to make arrangements for them to perform at the Tribal School where he was consulting. He saw their performance a second time after which we both agreed that our sons *had* to see the performance. We saw an ad in the paper that week for a performance by the Maxwell International Bahá'í School Diversity Dance Workshop to be held in town for a Naw Rúz (New Year) Celebration in April of that year.

Bahá'í?

I recognized the word. I had glimpsed commercials with faces of many colors and the word Bahá'í but hadn't paid attention. I had driven by a small ranch house in a run-down part of town that had "Bahá'í Center" on the sign. I read the powerful statement after 9/11 that had appeared in the local paper entitled "The Destiny of America and the Promise of World Peace:"

*At this time of world turmoil, the United States Bahá'í community offers a perspective on the destiny of America as the promoter of world peace.*

*More than a hundred years ago, Bahá'u'lláh, the founder of the Bahá'í Faith, addressing heads of state, proclaimed that the age of maturity for the entire human race had come. The unity of humankind was now to be established as the foundation of the great peace that would mark the highest stage in humanity's spiritual and social evolution. Revolutionary and world-shaking changes were therefore inevitable...*

*The American nation, Bahá'ís believe, will evolve through tests and trials to become a land of spiritual distinction and leadership, a champion of justice and unity among all peoples and nations, and a powerful servant of the cause of everlasting peace. This is the peace promised by God in the sacred texts of the world's religions...*

*Universal acceptance of the spiritual principle of the oneness of humankind is essential to any successful attempt to establish world peace.*

*Racism, one of the most baneful and persistent evils, is a major barrier to peace. The emancipation of women, the achievement of full equality of the sexes, is one of the most important, though less acknowledged, prerequisites of peace.*

*The inordinate disparity between rich and poor keeps the world in a state of instability, preventing the achievement of peace.*

*Unbridled nationalism, as distinguished from a sane and legitimate patriotism, must give way to a wider loyalty, to the love of humanity as a whole.*

*Religious strife... is a major obstacle to progress. The challenge facing the world's religious leaders is to contemplate... and to ask themselves whether they cannot...*

*submerge their theological differences... that will enable them to work together for the advancement of human understanding and peace...*

*During this hour of crisis, we affirm our abiding faith in the destiny of America. We know that the road to its destiny is long, thorny and tortuous, but we are confident that America will emerge from her trials undivided and undefeatable. – National Spiritual Assembly of the Baha'is of the United States*[11]

At the time, the country was in so much pain, reeling from the attack on its shores and on the verge of descending into paranoia, seeking retribution, creating new agencies, and imposing new laws on its populace, all in the hopes of preventing future terrorist activities on its soil. I read the above statement and was reassured and comforted. It brought tears to my eyes. The voice was powerful, and I felt the truth in its words.

I had believed that the human race was one and shouldn't be divided in hate by race, gender, religion, or nationalism. I believed that the earth was one home to the human race.

To see my deeply held but unspoken ideals in print, articulated so clearly and succinctly, touched something hidden in my heart. To read that humanity would become united and find the Most Great Peace were the most comforting and reassuring words I had ever seen.

As I read the statement about racism, I remembered when my family lived in Detroit, shortly after the 1967 riots, and my parents were selling our house to move to the suburbs. My family was part of the 'white flight' that took place, contributing to the demise of the beloved city of my childhood. I remembered opening the door and seeing a man and woman standing there, one black and one white. I had never seen an interracial couple before and looked at them in confusion and wonder. My mother greeted them and invited them in to look at the house. I watched my mother carefully, seeing how she treated this unusual pair. My mother acted like nothing was wrong or strange and was very welcoming and kind. As a child, through watching my mother, I concluded that skin color must make no difference and decided that people are just people, no matter our race. As I grew up, I learned that prejudice and racism were challenges to be overcome, within each of us and in our society.

My experiences of being thrust into the world of disability sharpened my sensitivity to prejudice of any kind. Experiencing life as a minority for the first time in my life since moving to Washington taught me a great deal about the emotional experience of being marginalized, left out, and unwanted, simply based on some external characteristic. The Bahá'í statements that racism, sexism, religious strife, and nationalism interfere with our living in peace and harmony, and that the answers to these problems are clear and spiritual, gave me a hope for the future of mankind that I had never felt before. The dances I had been witness to spoke with the same powerful, unifying voice.

It was clear to me that these Bahá'ís had something important to say.

We decided we would go to this Naw Rúz celebration, bring our sons, and see the full performance of the Diversity Dance Workshop.

The event was held in a big red barn. We walked in and saw a diverse crowd of people under the same roof. People were friendly and smiling. They were interacting and talking with one another. Hispanics, whites, blacks, and Native Americans were interacting and talking with one another. Our town was very segregated socially and economically, and it was unusual to see the 'races' mixing with one another let alone enjoying one another's company.

My family was welcomed, and no one avoided us because of my son's wheelchair, an experience which was all too familiar. We were invited to sit at a large, round table to watch the performance.

Even after having seen the dances three times before, I was again mesmerized by their power. They pinpointed the problems faced by mankind – prejudice, racism, sexism, poverty, abuse, drugs and alcohol – yet at the same time, showed how these problems could be overcome with love, unity, a celebration of differences, and oneness.

At the end of the performance, the dancers stood in a

line across the stage, and each one, in a strong voice, read a prayer from a different religion – Buddhism, Christianity, Hinduism, Native American traditions, Zoroastrian, Sikhism, Islam, Judaism, and the Bahá'í Faith. Each prayer was given importance and respect. Each one was read in a solemn voice.

I will never forget the moment the insight came upon me – I was hearing prayers from different religions, yet I only heard One voice. The religions were all *one*. I realized that the religions all came from the same source – they all came from God; there was really only *one religion* – the religion of God.

On that night, I came to the Bahá'í Faith and never left.

*Our human compassion binds us the one to the other – not in pity or patronizingly, but as human beings who have learnt how to turn our common suffering into hope for the future.*
Nelson Mandela[12]

# But it's an Organized Religion

However, as far as I knew, organized religion was not to be trusted. How could this one be any different? I didn't know of a religion whose basic teaching had not been somehow corrupted. Could this one be different? They read prayers from all the religions – does that mean they accept all of the religions? Would I find an 'us against them' mentality? Do they truly believe in unity, equality, and an end to prejudice?

My husband and I had been so moved by our experience at the performance that in spite of my reservations, we decided we would investigate and attend services. We mustered our courage, and, after driving by the Bahá'í Center for several Sundays, we finally entered.

In the small ranch house, the living room was set up for devotions. People of all ages were quietly sitting in chairs, many holding prayer books. There was a ramp leading up to the front door, a rarity that we didn't have to carry our son's wheelchair over some steps. An African-American man in a wheelchair was among the group – no one looked at our son with anything other than a smile. We had been used to feeling like a parade whenever we walked anywhere with spectators staring at the little boy in the small wheelchair, opening mouths, turning heads, and pointing fingers.

A sheet of readings was passed out, most from the Bahá'í writings but several from other religions, all focused on a theme. People took turns reading the passages and then offered their own prayers. Then, someone led singing. It felt like a warm and welcoming atmosphere without pressure or requirements to participate. After the devotions, everyone split up into classes, an adult class, youth, children, and a seeker class. My children happily went to the children's class, and my husband and I went to the 'seeker' class. There, we met a couple who would ultimately become our closest friends, and we spent the next seven months, every Sunday, grilling them, asking everything we could think of to discredit this organized religion.

The first thing I wanted to know about was clergy. Who is in charge? I was surprised to learn that the faith had no clergy. The woman who had led the devotions was a volunteer, and it was a rotating position. There were *no* clergy in this faith! How peculiar!

I learned about the principle of the independent investigation of the truth. It was up to me to find what was true, to read the writings, to develop my own relationship with God.

No clergyperson would be the interpreter of God's word or require me to admit my sins. There was no hell – hell was understood as 'distance from God.'

My 'sins' were between God and me:

*O SON OF BEING! Bring thyself to account each day ere thou art summoned to a reckoning; for death, unheralded, shall come upon thee and thou shalt be called to give account for thy deeds.*[13]

Children were to investigate for themselves as well, and it was not a given that a child born in a Bahá'í family would be Bahá'í. They would have to consciously choose for themselves.

Who is in charge if there are no clergy, I asked? There must be some leaders. Who develops the class materials and publishes the writings, supports people in distress, collects money and pays for buildings, develops resources, organizes the community – all of the myriad responsibilities of religious leaders?

I found out that in each area where there are at least nine adults, a Local Spiritual Assembly is elected to administer the affairs of the faith. The elections are held yearly without nominations or campaigns. The electorate studies the writings about the qualities needed for those who will serve, the names of all the adults from that locale are handed out on a piece of paper, and after prayer, and in silence, with no discussion, each Bahá'í checks off or circles nine names. The nine people with the most votes serve on the Local Assembly for one year.

National Spiritual Assemblies for each country are chosen in the same way by individuals elected to vote from every part of our country. In the United States, these individuals go to Wilmette, Illinois where the National Center is located, and after prayer, write down nine names. The nine Bahá'ís with the most votes serve for one year at the national level.

The Universal House of Justice is elected every five years by all the National Assemblies in the same manner. I thought that was an incredible name for the administrative body of the Bahá'í Faith. Justice, yes, Justice. It is all about Justice, universally, for everyone.

I couldn't imagine that a system like this actually existed.

*O SON OF SPIRIT! The best beloved of all things in My sight is Justice… Verily justice is My gift to thee and the sign of My loving-kindness. Set it then before thine eyes.*[14]

I had been disgusted by the corruption of the democratic system, the money and greed, the negativity and hatred, the division and extreme partisanship in Washington D.C. The Bahá'í system was so different from anything I had ever heard of in either secular life or in my understanding of how people became leaders of other religions.

This truly was a brand new idea. Every person was involved, and every vote truly counted. For those elected to serve on Local and National Assemblies, I read the following guidance:

*They should approach their task with extreme humility, and endeavor, by their open-mindedness, their high sense of justice and duty, their candor, their modesty, their entire devotion to the welfare and interests of the friends, the Cause, and humanity... They must, at all times, avoid the spirit of exclusiveness, the atmosphere of secrecy, free themselves from a domineering attitude, and banish all forms of prejudice and passion from their deliberations.*[15]

In direct contrast, when decisions were made or laws were passed in Washington, I felt revulsion as one opposing side did everything in its power to undermine the other, to tear apart decisions, and to work against them in every way possible. How were we ever to know whether decisions or laws had any merit? How were we to learn if ideas were not fully supported and implemented once they'd been voted in?

In this fascinating Bahá'í system, decisions which were made by the Assembly were reached after consultation and a vote with a majority rule. The minority was to support the decision without reservation and make sure the will of the Assembly was carried out without resentment, anger, bitterness – rather with heartfelt support. In this way, it would become clear whether the decision was a good one or not. The Assembly would learn and would use this new learning to inform their future decisions.

*And, when they are called upon to arrive at a certain decision, they should, after dispassionate, anxious and cordial consultation, turn to God in prayer, and with earnestness and conviction and courage record their vote and abide by the voice of the majority...* [16]

I learned that God was viewed as an unknowable essence, the creator of the universe Who we can only know by His reflection in the perfect mirrors, the manifestations or prophets of God who convey God's teachings to us. How could humans know or understand the Creator of something as immense and unexplainable as the universe? How could a painting know the painter, a table know the carpenter? That made sense to me.

I learned that Bahá'ís believed each religion was a successive chapter in the one religion of God, and that God sent messengers to guide and teach His creation based on our needs borne out of time and place. The needs of humans 2000 years ago were starkly different from the needs of today. They had a song to help the children remember all of the known manifestations:

*Krishna, Buddha, Zoroaster*
*Abraham, Moses, Christ*
*Mohammed, the Báb, Bahá'u'lláh*

*The spirit's the same.*
*Bahá'u'lláh teaches for today*
*Asks us to look to the spirit*
*Not to worship the name.*[17]

Bahá'u'lláh was the manifestation for today, the Glory of God, who came at a time when humans were entering their adolescence and needed help to proceed to their next stage in development – adulthood and the maturation and unification of humankind.

We are ready to unite. Humans now have the ability to be in contact with every part of the world; the internet connects us, travel makes any place on earth about a day away, and English is being taught more and more around the world. We are contracting into a neighborhood and beginning to be able to see others as our fellow citizens.

Baha'u'llah came to help us toward world peace in which humans will live as one family in a "just, global society."[18]

This all sounded very good, but I argued that each manifestation said they were the only way. And what about the ones who said they were the last and final way? Did Baha'u'llah say that He was the last messenger from God?

I discovered that this was not the case – Baha'u'llah said there will be other manifestations after Him, the first not before one thousand years. And that God will never leave

His creation without assistance. Manifestations will always be sent as humankind evolves and needs change. Each said they were the only way because there is only One God and One religion – the religion of God. The spirit of each manifestation is the same.

Yes, I knew this, intuitively. After hearing the voices in each prayer from the different religions, I knew that there was really only One religion with One God who just happened to be known by different names – Yahweh, Elohim, Creator, Jehovah, Allah, Brahma, Takashana…

*No matter how innumerable its risings, there is but one sun, and upon it depends the life of all things… And this Faith -- the Faith of Him Whom God will make manifest -- in its turn, together with all the Revelations gone before it, have as their object the Manifestation destined to succeed it. And the latter, no less than all the Revelations preceding it, prepare the way for the Revelation which is yet to follow. The process of the rise and setting of the Sun of Truth will thus indefinitely continue -- a process that hath had no beginning and will have no end.*[19]

So what about the corruption, the hypocrisy, the hatred spewed by some of the religions?

It was explained that each religion has a springtime and flowering. It goes into summer and bears fruit, and then comes the fall and winter when the religion no longer serves its purpose and becomes corrupted by man. It needs to be refreshed by a new springtime, a new manifestation, and a new messenger with updated laws and teachings for that day. Yet the underlying principles are all the same.

I could not find anything wrong. For each question I brought up, they had answers that made sense both logically and emotionally.

But what about science? Most religions denigrate science and deny evolution. Would the Bahá'í Faith do the same?

I discovered that one of the principles of the faith was the harmony of science and religion. I was excited to read the following:

*Bahá'ís reject the notion that there is an inherent conflict between science and religion. Instead they believe science and religion are two systems of knowledge. Each operating within its own sphere, they are fundamentally in harmony, mutually reinforcing, and are both necessary to advance civilization.*

*The Faith teaches that religion without science soon degenerates into superstition and fanaticism, while science without religion becomes merely the instrument of crude materialism – and unchecked material progress will never lead to true prosperity.*

*Science and religion both describe reality, and reality is one. It is not possible for something to be scientifically false and religiously true. Contradictions are attributed to human fallibility. Science trains our minds to discover hidden realities. Religion helps us uncover the meaning and proper uses of scientific discovery...* [20]

A faith that would not require me to relinquish my logical mind, to give up my love of science, to ignore the evidence of evolution!

I learned that there was a means to end prejudice – a scourge on humanity. I asked my husband, who is also a singer-songwriter and guitar player, to put one of my favorite Bahá'í writings to music:

*O CHILDREN OF MEN! Know ye not why We created you all from the same dust? That no one should exalt himself over the other. Ponder at all times in your hearts how ye were created. Since We have created you all from one same substance it is incumbent on you to be even as one soul, to walk with the same feet, eat with the same mouth and dwell in the same land, that from your inmost being, by your deeds and actions, the signs of oneness and the essence of detachment may be made manifest...* [21]

I would memorize these words to remember them when I was confronted with my own prejudice against people who were so different from me, foreign, frightening, unknown.

I worked to open my heart to develop friendships

with people I would not have normally befriended. I worked to make 'Namaste' (what I understood as seeing God in those I met) my way of being.

I learned more about the Bahá'í principles: the equality of men and women, economic principles that discussed the lessening of the extremes of wealth and poverty and how to achieve this, compulsory universal education, a world language so everyone could communicate, methods of governance, consultation, the ways and means to unite the planet while celebrating the unique languages, cultures, arts, the wonderful diversity that makes up our human race, the protection of our earth and how to live sustainably, a system of administration with prayer-filled elections, no nominations or campaigns.

In the Bahá'í Faith, I found a blueprint, an instruction manual for how to live in this world, how to develop my own relationship with God, prayer, fasting, work as worship, service to humanity. I learned about the existence and purpose of the soul, the unity of science and religion in understanding evolution, the afterlife and the countless worlds of God.

I learned about other religions, more now about Judaism than I had from my Jewish grandparents. I learned to appreciate and love Jesus and Mohammad. I learned that I could raise my children in a world assured to reach the Greater Peace, the kingdom of heaven on earth. I found that as a member of this human family, I could develop the courage to cross boundaries, to discover new spiritual truths, to find internal peace and a reason to hope for my future, my children's future, and the future of the planet and mankind.

I learned to try to understand the seeming coincidences in my own life as signs and tokens from God. I tried to live consciously and aware of people who crossed my path, events occurring around me, opportunities presented to me, and choices to be made.

*He who learns must suffer. And even in our sleep pain that cannot forget falls drop by drop upon the heart, and in our own despair, against our will, comes wisdom to us by the awful grace of God.* – Aeschylus[22]

# WHY DO WE SUFFER?

But most of all, the Bahá'í Faith answered my questions about suffering.

I learned that God provides the motion with which we move, but we provide the direction in which we go. The choices to turn left or right are ours. Many of mankind's decisions *cause* suffering.

I had been disgusted that bake sales and fundraisers by families of children with SMA were needed to support research into treatments and cures while billions and billions of dollars were readily available to pay for war and destruction. I remembered the fundraiser held at the Unitarian Church that we had belonged to in order to fund the experimental drug study and our stay in New Jersey.

Would my family and I have suffered so much if discrimination against disabled individuals were not so entrenched, if paraplegics had not had to crawl up the steps of the Lincoln Memorial to gain access? If looks and the way society defined beauty did not lead to rejection, prejudice, and being simply left out? The Americans with Disabilities Act was not passed until 1990, and from my youth, I remembered that there were separate schools for children in wheelchairs. I did not want my son to be marginalized when he had so much to offer this world.

I thought cancer would be cured by now, toxins wouldn't be polluting our environment, and poverty wouldn't be so widespread if the choices man made had been different. The horrible prejudice that resulted in genocide, oppression, and injustice was a function of the choices made by man.

God couldn't give His creation free will and then prevent His creatures from using it when they went in the wrong direction. I thought about how my children learned the most from their own mistakes, yet I still always provided guidance and assistance to them, just like God did for humanity. I concluded that most of our suffering is manmade. I read the following Bahá'í quotation and saw the sense in it:

*There is, unfortunately, no way that one can force his own good upon a man. The element of free will is there, and all we believers -- and even the Manifestation of God Himself -- can do is to offer the truth to mankind. If the people of the world persist, as they seem to be doing, in their blind materialism, they must bear the consequences in a prolongation of our present condition, and even a worsening of it.*[23]

What about events not within the purview of our free will? Did human choice somehow result in the fact that my husband's and my DNA both carry the SMA gene? I couldn't think of how this would be possible. This seemed to be a random fluke yet somehow destined to happen. Why would this kind of suffering happen to people?

What about hurricanes, earthquakes, tsunamis...?

The answer I received was that it is through suffering that we develop virtues, come to know our spiritual natures, become aware of spiritual truths, and grow and strengthen ourselves.

The question I eventually came to ask was not why do we suffer, rather what should I do with my suffering? What choices do I now make? Do I become bitter and angry and withdraw from the world? Or do I reach out with compassion, learn, and help others?

Does the predicament of our family help people learn to accept differences? Does it help people learn to look past the physical and see the character, the spirit? Do we work to make changes in society for how people are treated?

I already knew that it was through challenges and hard work that I learned and made progress in my school and work. I remembered the difficulty of making it through college and my doctorate, the grinding work to complete my dissertation.

Why would progressing spiritually require any less work? It was only through suffering that I found God and discovered my spiritual path. I would have had no reason to wonder about anything beyond what I could see were it not for my own suffering.

I thought of my son as 'he who brought God to the family.'

I learned that it is through suffering that one develops spiritual qualities – empathy, strength, perseverance, stamina, compassion, patience, gratitude, generosity, resignation, serenity, forgiveness...

I looked at the world around me and thought that physical comforts and riches rarely lead to wisdom, maturity, or spiritual truths. Through the lens of suffering, one is able to see more clearly and become open to truths the physical world can blind one to. I thought of my own challenges throughout life and knew that as I faced each one, I learned, grew, and changed.

I thought about the suffering of the prophets of God – Buddha, Jesus, Mohammed, the Bahá'í prophets, the Báb, and Bahá'u'lláh. Each one suffered immeasurably yet was characterized by the greatest virtues.

One of my favorite quotes was put on our refrigerator

to remind me of the answer to my questions about suffering:

*The more you plough and dig the ground the more fertile it becomes. The more you cut the branches of a tree the higher and stronger it grows. The more you put the gold in the fire the purer it becomes. The more you sharpen the steel by grinding the better it cuts. Therefore, the more sorrows one sees the more perfect one becomes. That is why, in all times, the Prophets of God have had tribulations and difficulties to withstand. The more often the captain of a ship is in the tempest and difficult sailing the greater his knowledge becomes. Therefore I am happy that you have had great tribulations and difficulties. For this I am very happy -- that you have had many sorrows. Strange it is that I love you and still I am happy that you have sorrows.*[24]

Through my study of the Bahá'í Faith, I learned that each religion addressed the question of suffering. Writers, leaders, peacemakers, people from all walks of life have struggled with suffering. I collected quotes to help deepen my understanding.

Taoism: *But whether or not we ascertain what is the true nature of this soul, it matters but little to the soul itself. For once coming into this material shape, it runs its course until it is exhausted. To be harassed by the wear and tear of life, and to be driven along without possibility of arresting one's course, -- is not this pitiful indeed?*[25]

Buddhism: *Birth is suffering; Decay is suffering;*

*Death is suffering; Sorrow, Lamentation, Pain, Grief, and Despair, are suffering; not to get what one desires, is suffering...*[26]

Hinduism: *Sorrow and suffering, trial and endurance, are a part of the Hindu ideal of a Perfect Life of righteousness...*[27]

Judaism: *And thou shalt remember all the way which the LORD thy God hath led thee these forty years in the wilderness, that He might afflict thee, to prove thee, to know what was in thy heart, whether thou wouldest keep His commandments, And He afflicted thee, and suffered thee to hunger, and fed thee with manna, which thou knewest not, neither did thy fathers know; that He might make thee know that man doth not live by bread only, but by every thing that proceedeth out of the mouth of the LORD doth man live.*[28]

Christianity: *Fear none of those things which thou shalt suffer: behold, the devil shall cast some of you into prison, that ye may be tried; and ye shall have tribulation ten days: be thou faithful unto death, and I will give thee a crown of life.*[29]

Islam: *...to be firm and patient, in pain (or suffering) and adversity, and throughout all periods of panic. Such are the people of truth, the Allah-fearing.*[30]

Sikhism: *The thorn of egotism is embedded deep within them. The more they walk away, the deeper it pierces them, and the more they suffer in pain...*[31]

Native American tradition: *We live, we die, and like the grass and the trees, renew ourselves from the soft earth of the grave. Stones crumble and decay, faiths grow old and they are forgotten, but the new beliefs are born. The faith of the villages is dust now...but it will grow again...like the trees.*[32]

# ACCEPTANCE

I was content with the answers to all of my questions. I accepted that Bahá'u'lláh was the Divine Manifestation for today. I learned about and believed in past Messengers – Jesus, Buddha, Mohammed, Moses, Abraham, Zoroaster.

I came to know other Bahá'ís – warm, loving, open people from all walks of life, working to build the Greater Peace, to see an end to prejudice and hatred, discord and disunity. Working hard to use the tools they were given in the countless writings of the Báb (the forerunner and Gate of the Faith), Bahá'u'lláh, his son 'Abdul-Bahá (the Exemplar of the Faith), and his grandson, Shoghi Effendi (the Guardian of the Faith).

The Bahá'ís I knew were not always successful in meeting the standards taught in the writings, but they tried to implement the teachings in the best way they could, always learning from mistakes and *trying* to be Bahá'ís.

I had found my way. I had found a way to integrate God into my life, a way to understand the totality of the universe, the soul, the afterlife, science, religion, suffering...

I developed a newfound optimism for the future for my children and all of humanity and now knew how to raise them in the world in which I found myself. I found a goal, a body of work for life-long study, a way to embrace all of humanity and God.

I wanted to live my life *becoming* a Bahá'í.

I thought about this for several weeks. Could I become a Bahá'í? Could I live up to the standards for behavior? Could I change habits, ways of thinking, ways of being?

Would I alienate my family and lose my close relationship with them? I had been an atheist in a family of nonbelievers. How would becoming a Bahá'í change my life?

I would try to say daily prayers; I would try to fast for nineteen days from sunrise to sunset; I would try to view my work as worship; I would try to cross established boundaries and get to know people who lived in different worlds, with different lifestyles, with different beliefs and cultures and try to see them as my relatives.

How could I go from seeing religion as a crutch to actually joining one? To seeing religion as something that inspired hatred and cruelty to something that could uplift and change the lot of man?

I had investigated for myself. I had read. I had questioned. I was ready. I would become a Bahá'í. I could raise my children surrounded by people who worked to accept differences and unique talents – unity in diversity. In this world they were trying to create, disability would not preclude my son from being an active part of the community.

Wait, my husband responded. Wait for me! He wasn't ready yet; he wanted to know if Baha'u'llah was a Buddha. He was a Buddhist and thought he heard the same voice in both the Buddhist and Baha'i writings, but he wasn't sure.

He also wondered if he could ever live up to the standards set by the Faith, the focus on virtues, consultation rather than confrontation, love for humanity.

I told him I would wait a week, but then I was committed to becoming a Bahá'í. He could make his own decision. I would not pressure him. This was something I wanted to do for myself. I would wait one week.

A week passed. My husband and I were standing in the potluck line at the Bahá'í Center when someone who had become a friend said, "You really like the Bahá'ís, don't you? Remember, we are no different than everyone else in the world, crazy as the rest of them. The only difference is we are trying to *be* Bahá'ís."

Once he heard this, my husband decided to take a leap of faith. He did not have to live up to some unreachable measure of virtue and behavior. All he had to do was try. Together, we would become Bahá'ís.

It was only a week following our decision that my husband was given a book written by Bahá'u'lláh entitled *The Seven Valleys and the Four Valleys*. In it, he heard Buddha's voice and read about the journey through the valleys of suffering toward detachment and enlightenment. He knew that Bahá'u'lláh and the Buddha were of the same spirit and both were of God.

Together, we would begin our new journey through challenges and heartache, through joys and adventures, working towards helping our fellow humans, in our small area of the world, understand the oneness of the human race.

We would help our sons grow up, facing discrimination, disability, achieving successes, finding love, having broken hearts, through crises and victories, knowing they were not alone in this world and would always have God's love surrounding them.

I watched my youngest son graduate high school, enter college, develop friends and skills, find his own gifts and talents, and hold his girlfriend's hand as they strolled together across the courtyard, she walking and he in his wheelchair, knowing the truth behind the voice, "He will be teased in the school yard, and he will be married."

I went from atheist to believer, a journey through suffering, to the Bahá'í Faith.

*The Guest House*

*This being human is a guest house.*
*Every morning a new arrival.*

*A joy, a depression, a meanness,*
*some momentary awareness comes*
*as an unexpected visitor.*

*Welcome and entertain them all!*
*Even if they're a crowd of sorrows,*
*who violently sweep your house*
*empty of its furniture,*
*still, treat each guest honorably.*
*He may be clearing you out*
*for some new delight.*

*The dark thought, the shame, the malice,*
*Meet them at the door laughing,*
*And invite them in.*

*Be grateful for whoever comes,*
*Because each has been sent*
*As a guide from beyond.*

-- Rumi[33]

# RESOURCES

Families of SMA (Spinal Muscular Atrophy):
http://www.fsma.org/

Muscular Dystrophy Association: http://mda.org/

Ocean – Free Library of the World's Religious Literature for
download: http://bahai-education.org/

Baha'i Faith – Official Website of the Bahá'ís of the United
States: http://www.bahai.us/  1-800-22-UNITE

Bahá'í Faith – The International Website of the Bahá'ís of the
World: http://www.bahai.org/

Diversity Dance Company:
http://www.ajusticenetwork.org/ddc-about.shtml

Hidden Word #68 O Children of Men, arranged by David
Edward Walker on http:// www.youtube.com

# Works Cited

1 Achebe, Chinua. "Chinua Achebe." *Goodreads*. Goodreads, Inc. Web. 13 Aug 2013.
<http://www.goodreads.com/quotes/412390-when-suffering-knocks-at-your-door-and-you-say-tmye>.

2 Eliot, George. "George Eliot." *Wikiquote*. Wikimedia, 16 Jul 2013. Web. 14 Aug 2013.
<http://en.wikiquote.org/wiki/George_Eliot>.

3 Nietzsche, Friedrich. "Friedrich Nietzsche Quotes." *Search Quotes*. SearchQuotes, Web. 13 Aug 2013.
<http://www.searchquotes.com/quotation/To_live_is_to_suffer,_to_survive_is_to_find_some_meaning_in_the_suffering./290712/>.

4 Churchill, Winston. "Winston Churchill 1864-1965."*aboutwinstonchurchill.com*. Winston Churchill Quotes, 13 May 2013. Web. 34 Aug 2013.
<http://aboutwinstonchurchill.com/72/2013/05/we-shall-

draw-from-the-heart-of-suffering-itself-the-means-of-inspiration-and-survival-winston-churchill/>.

5 Rumi. "Mindfulness and Poetry for Transformation." *Mindful Living Programs*. Mindful Living Programs. Web. 13 Aug 2013. <http://www.mindfullivingprograms.com/poetry.php>.

6 "Providence and Suffering." *torah.org*. Project Genesis, Inc. Web. 13 Aug 2013. <http://www.torah.org/features/spirfocus/suffering.html>.

7 Wright, Frances. "Frances Wright Quotes." *BrainyQuote*. Book Rags Media Network. Web. 7 Sep 2013.< http://www.brainyquote.com/quotes/authors/f/frances_wright .html>.

8 Coelho, Paul. "My Heart is Afraid to Suffer." *Paul Coelho's Blog*. Wordpress, 14 Feb 2012. Web. 13 Aug 2013. <http://paulocoelhoblog.com/2012/02/14/our-hear/>.

9 Dickens, Charles. "Great Expectations, chapter 59." *Literature.org: The Online Literature Library*. Knowledge Matters Ltd. Web. 13 Aug 2013.

<http://www.literature.org/authors/dickens-charles/great-expectations/chapter-59.html>.

10 Bray, Libba. "Libba Bray." *Goodreads*. Goodreads, Inc. Web. 13 Aug 2013.
<http://www.goodreads.com/quotes/60443-tmye-is-an-ancient-tribal-proverb-i-once-heard-in>.

11 "The Destiny of America and the Promise of World Peace." *Bahá'í Faith: Official Website of the Bahá'ís of the United States*. National Spiritual Assembly of the Bahá'ís of the United States. Web. 13 Aug 2013.
<http://www.bahai.us/destiny-of-america/>.

12 Mandela, Nelson. "Nelson Mandela Quotes." *BrainyQuote*. Book Rags Media Network. Web. 13 Aug 2013.
<http://www.brainyquote.com/quotes/authors/n/nelson_mandela_2.html>.

13 Bahá'u'lláh. "The Hidden Words of Bahá'u'lláh, 31." *Bahá'í Reference Library*. Bahá'í International Community. Web. 13 Aug 2013.

<http://reference.bahai.org/en/t/b/HW/hw-32.html>.

14 Bahá'u'lláh. "The Hidden Words of Bahá'u'lláh, 2." *Bahá'í Reference Library*. Bahá'í International Community. Web. 13 Aug 2013. < http://reference.bahai.org/en/t/b/HW/hw-3.html>.


15 Shoghi Effendi. "Duties of Elected Representatives: Letter of 23 February 1924," *Bahá'í Administration*. U. S. Bahá'í Publishing Trust, 1974. 63-64. Print. <http://reference.bahai.org/en/t/se/BA/>.


16 ibid.


17 " Bahá'í i Peace CD Lyrics." *Shell Harbour Bahá'í Community*. The Local Spiritual Assembly of the Bahá'ís of Shell Harbour, NSW, Australia. Web. 13 Aug 2013. <http://Shellharbour.nsw.bahai.org.au/Download/lyrics.pdf>.


18 "Q & A." *Bahá'í Faith: Official Website of the Bahá'ís of the United States*. National Spiritual Assembly of the *Bahá'ís* of the United States. Web. 7 Sep 2013. <http://mig.bahai.us/Q-A>.

19 The Báb. "Selections From the Writings of the Báb."
*Bahá'í Reference Library*. Bahá'í International Community.
Web. 7 Sep 2013. <http://reference.bahai.org/en/t/tb/SWB/>.


20 "Harmony of Science and Religion." *Bahá'í Faith:
Official Website of the Bahá'ís of the United States*. National
Spiritual Assembly of the Bahá'ís of the United States.Web.
13 Aug 2013. <http://www.bahai.us/welcome/principles-and-
practices/harmony-of-science-and-religion/>.


21 Bahá'u' lláh. "The Hidden Words of Bahá'u'lláh,
68." *Bahá'í Reference Library*. Bahá'í International
Community. Web. 13 Aug 2013.
<http://reference.bahai.org/en/t/b/HW/hw-69.html>.


22 Aeschylus. "Aeschylus Quotes." *BrainyQuote*. Book Rags
Media Network. Web. 7 Sep 2013.
<http://www.brainyquote.com/quotes/authors/a/aeschylus.ht
ml>.

23 Shoghi Effendi. "Unfolding Destiny: Letter of 13 October
1947." *Bahá'í Reference Library*. Bahá'í International
Community. Web. 13 Aug 2013.
<http://reference.bahai.org/en/t/se/UD/ud-609.html>.

24 'Abdu'l-Bahá . "`Abdu'l-Bahá on Suffering and Tests."
*Bahá'í Topics: An Information Resource of the Bahá'í
International Community*. Bahá'í International Community.
Database. 13 Aug 2013. <http://info.bahai.org/article-1-3-4-
7.html>.


25 Tao, Chuangtse. Legge, J., translator. *Lin Yutang
tr. Ocean - Free Library of World's Religious Literature*.
Database. 13 Aug 2013. <http://bahai-education.org/>.


26 Buddha . "The Eightfold Path." *Word. Ocean - Free
Library of World's Religious Literature*. Database. 13 Aug
2013. <http://bahai-education.org/>.


27 Ramayana. Dutt, Romesh, translator. *Epic of Rama,
Prince of India* (1899). *Ocean - Free Library of World's
Religious Literature*. Database. 13 Aug 2013. <http://bahai-
education.org/>.


28 "Devarim (Deuteronomy)." *Torah Law. Ocean - Free
Library of World's Religious Literature*. Database. 14 Aug
2013. <http://bahai-education.org/>.

29 "Revelations." *King James Bible* 2:10. *Ocean - Free Library of World's Religious Literature.* Database. 13 Aug 2013. <http://bahai-education.org/>.


30 *Quran* Surah 2. 177. *Ocean - Free Library of World's Religious Literature.* Database. 14 Aug 2013. <http://bahai-education.org/>.


31 *Shri Guru Granth Sahib,* Section 4.Sohila. *Ocean - Free Library of World's Religious Literature.* Database. 13 Aug 2013. <http://bahai-education.org/>.


32 Chief Joseph. "Inspirational Quotes: Traditional Knowledge and Education." *California Indian Education.* www.calie.org. Web. 7 Sep 2013. <http://www.californiaindianeducation.org/inspire/traditional />.


33 Rumi, Jalal al-Din. "The Guest House." Translated by Coleman Barks. *The Essential Rumi.* San Francisco: Harper, 2004. 109. Print.